Who is the Public Poem? Not a what. The Public Poem which I invented in 1966-67 in Brussels is a person in the street; in this case my person. Ceci n'est pas une Performance, my character says. Because the STREET is his milieu, his text, his poem, his grand theater. However it is not experienced as such because the pressure of economics, the signs of consumption, numb us. Creative thought is dimmed, passive consumers are easily manipulated. The "polis" has vanished. Yet the city is still the focus of signs, the crossings of the most diverse humanity. We need to appropriate it- to write it! In our highly mediatized culture and virtual cities, the action of our bodies in the street-shocks! My body is not a hypothetical body or the mythical body of body-art. As a visual poet in the sixties, I asked myself, "Why not write on the city like a page?" Instead of appropriating mass media signs in a visual poetry page, appropriate street materials! When

I do a Public Poem, my body is the hand that writes, with physical effort I push the writing before me in the street, generating a grammar and a semantics of the street. Using graphic and phonemic signs (masks, materials, linguistic signs), I point to an underlying city-text: both "polis" and dream-place. A poetics of the street grows visible. When I write the street, a pathway is opened into the unpredictable dimension of social reality: passers-by, accidents, interferences. The Public Poem, unlike performances, takes place in the uncategorized space of the city; it cannot be "consumed" as art. It poses a radical question to its audience, the public at large. Who is it? a terrorist, a publicist, a madman? I invented the form in an era of intense public involvement: the Vietnam War, feminism, black liberation Today a fresh context reanimates public awareness-- "occupy Wall Street", Arab Spring, social media. Art meets politics meets dream: the Polis. And the Public Poem!

The first "public poem" was more of a political manifestation than a poetic form. I had fled the Vietnam War draft when the FBI had come knocking at my door in Greenwich Village in '66. It was Christmas of '67 now in the downtown shopping center of Brussels and I just wanted to make the NAME concrete in the midst of the indifferent Xmas cheer: human-sized letters made of crushed newspaper wrapped in surgical tape splattered with blood-red liquid--a menacing presence nobody could ignore. The letters swayed and shook in the wintry wind and the snow flurries. Look, someone said, it's V I E T N A M, that's good! No, said somebody else, it's a publicity stunt. About what? said the first person. It's about the war! My heart swelled. The word had become present.

I did the 🯅 GOD Public Poem in Brussels in 1968; it was a clearer fusion of page and street, of letter and human form. The meaning was simple enough: with the g in my right hand and the d in my left, and the "Poet" as cipher or 🯅 null, I bracketed one "class" of site after the other throughout the City to portray the disappearance of GOD and the City as God in His place: the RR station which breathed the citizens in at 8 am, the Cathedral, the Museum of Fine Arts, a Funeral Parlor, the Stock Exchange a Work Site, "Nature" (the Park), the great Galeries de la Reine as "Commerce" etc. The "poem" was still static and solitary, but the sense of a "reading" of the street more manifest. These were my first steps in an attempt to create a literacy of the street.

A MADRID (in Madrid) 1969, was the first fully realized Public Poem— I felt the street-page under my fingers (the legs, the bodies, the hands, of my "team") holding the pen inscribing the letters about the city. A MADRID underwent permutations like the operation of any concrete poem: RIADA flowed down the street stretching into "stream"; ARIDA, "arid" begged at the gates of a high-society church; MARIA descended the underground mens' latrines (led by a nubile girl) much to the hilarity of macho Madrilenians—and reemerged as RIMA just to show it was a poem; ARMA, "weapon", strutted by Franco's Parliament permutating to AMAR, "love", as soon as the Guardia Civil (of Lorca fame) began to nip at our heels; and DADA invaded the reactionary literary café El Gijon. I believe my friend Ignacio Gomez de Liano, Virgilian guide in Fascist Madrid, today Spain's most eminent philosopher, particularly enjoyed this thumbing of the literary nose..

My great friend Paul De Vree invited me back from Spain to the Knokke Poetry Festival in 1970, where I did my Public Baptismal Poem, POEMX. One by one I dipped the human-sized foam rubber letters in the salty North Sea with ritual gestures: P O E M X--until they were so soaked that they were too heavy to lift. By poetc osmosis World was absorbed into Word and this literal rite wrote the waves until the waves became writing and the gulls and the wind metaphor and a new poetics by this baptism was born: POEMX.

In 1971 in Madrid, city dynamics played a more active role in PALABRAS FRAGILES, "fragile words", which I staged again with Ignacio. Two transparent sheets of plastic stretched across a busy street with the words written on them, effectively arresting a basic city code: traffic. Unheard of in fascist Spain! The poetic "Word" was manifest in its fragility. Cars piled up—the inevitable occured: with a roar of motors amid cries of "Olé!" the traffic burst this hymen with macho brio completing the text of the Public Poem—the virginity of the Word in the City

In 1972 the City of Pamplona show-cased experimental art for the first time in Spain. Artists arrived worldwide, I returned from Belgium to do a PUBLIC PUNCTUATION POEM. The concept was simple: giant punctuation marks stuck on monuments (Hemingway), Parliament, public urinals, the national theater etc. connecting them in a city-wide "Sentence" of political satire. A thousand people followed-- the secret police threatened to shoot if the "demonstration" were not stopped! So I distributed the symbols to anyone who so desired! Hundreds of punctuations ran amok in the city!

Right after the Pamplona riot, I did the CHOMSKY GENERATIVE GRAMMAR PUBLIC POEM in Brussels in 1972. It was a cool action in contrast, more conceptual. Inspired by Chomsky, grammarian and political theorist, I wanted to show how the deep grammar of a street sentence could be labelled like a written sentence. Gluing human-sized grammatical symbols down a street, I framed bank, stores, people, police, illustrating that in a "deep" reading "people" was the direct object and not the subject they supposed, "commerce" was the verb qualified by the adverb "police", the subject an abstract noun "money" etc. I was astonished by the attitude of the Belgians; unlike the enthusiastic participation of the Spaniards, my fellow-citizens averted their gaze as from something faintly indecorous. The policeman whom I had impatiently awaited for a touch of drama was officiously polite but unshakeably firm, and unlike his armed Spanish cousins, inescapable. A "soft" repression, but efficacious..

On my return to Manhattan in 1974, the town I grew up in, I did the CAT & MAUS Public Poem, using cartoon characters because they are bigger than life and they alone can survive in Schizocity. New Yorkers are the purest of speech-figures in this floating world: they speak in cartoon-balloons in the subway and participate in the same substance—packets of air! I wore an Ignatz the Mouse mask and Nela, my then wife, a Krazy Kat mask, and we conversed by means of giant speech-balloons, raised and lowered one after the other in ritualistic gestures like Noh personages, overlooking Madison Square Garden, a natural theater with its huge, unwitting audience. Our conversation consisted of a mish-mash of TV clichés & topical chatter & canned poetry, and we did achieve communion with our fellow-denizens!

The City of Bonn invited me to do a Public Poem for the Beethoven Bicentennial in 1975. Marc Dachy, Dada Doc, joined me (spat on by an enraged music lover!). Giant notes from B's best-known musical phrases, not as signs for music but of music, so familiar that they have become speech-music, from da-da-da duh of the Emperor or the Moonlight Sonata. The blown-up, cartoon notes, instead of contributing to the "cultural" enhancement of the city for financial reasons, gave a subversive reading of the city via a revolutionary B: we sank the EROICA from Kennedy Bridge in the epic Rhein; Berlin Freedom Street got bars from the FUNERAL MARCH; EMPEROR variations for the Commerce Bank, boldest bar for Maximilianus; PASTORALE at the fruit & veggie market, the NINTH at grand Münsterplatz, "JOY!JOY!" on the vast Dresdener Bank, Violins I & II for the huge Kaufhof, and "MOONLIGHT" on sooty factory walls: police wagons and the enraged music-lover awaited us in FINALE!

The "PROUST PUBLIC POEM" was enacted in Paris in 1975, again in collaboration with Dada-drunk friend Marc Dachy. Paris for me is saturated with scenes from Marcel Proust; I had to bring Him back into the city and the times. We unloaded a giant TV screen in the middle of the Saint-Germain-des-Près square plus a giant cut-out of Marcel Proust. An interview was held by means of great cartoon speech-balloons between the Great Writer (with Marc) in the center of the square and me in the TV frame- we were linked by a black elastic (psychic link) ribbon hundreds of feet long which effectively blocked all traffic. We discussed current events, TV shows, Marcel's life. Traffic piled up people laughed, cursed, gaped. I felt that this insertion of le petit Marcel was successful in its inclusion of the Parisian community: arresting the dynamic of the city allowed a space/time gap for this dream-figure to exist. The arrival of three police vans was conclusive-Proust was taken seriously!

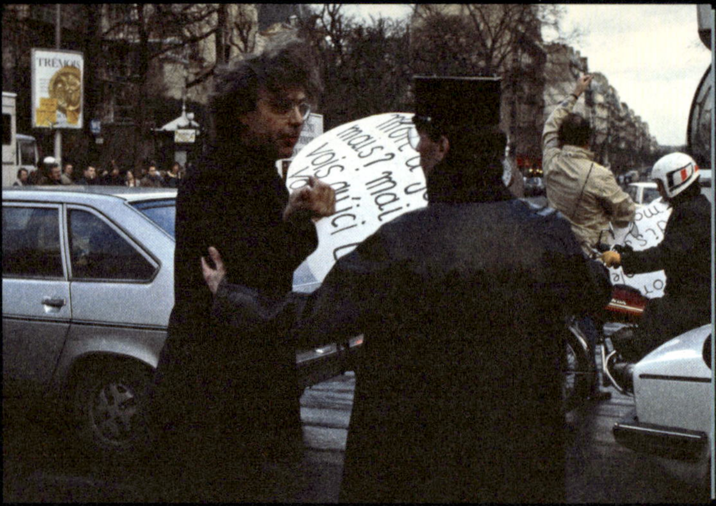
TRÉMOIS
mais? mai
vois ici

à la béatitu-
de? un monde
différent fondé
sur

h! cher Marcel
je pouvais
éteindre pour toi

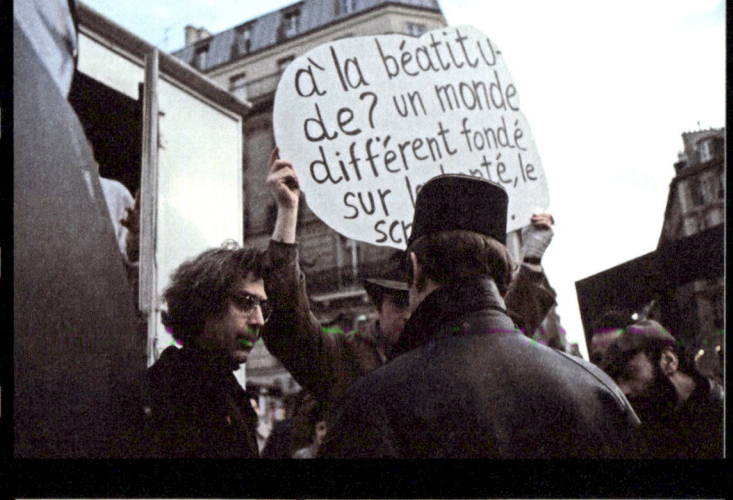

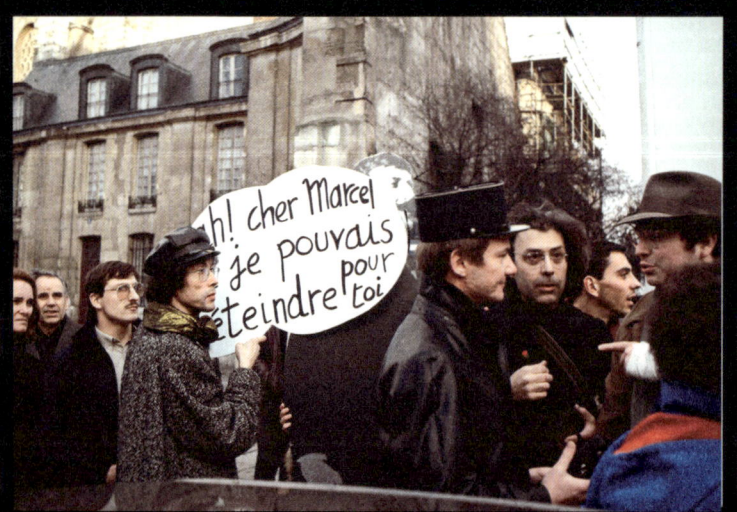

In 1991 the German "Literatur-Haus" invited me to do my TEUTONIC PUBLIC POEM in Berlin. Six masked characters (Freud, Marx, Madonna, Hitler, Donald Duck & Saddam Hussein) on sofas with beer bottles in a kitsch livingroom on wheels- no walls except for the front in the form of a huge tv screen, through which they gazed at the street crowds gawking at them as the wagon was propelled through the streets, music blaring 1930's beer keller tunes. In the middle of the biggest crossroads of the city, we blocked the wheels, Donald and Hitler remained in the livingroom while the others scattered to the corners of the giant square, warlike sound-effects were set off, and all the characters raised and lowered speech-balloons in a conversation on German culture, history and eroticism--until the police cars arrived and repressed us as I hoped! The grip of the huge policeman left marks on my arm for a week!

In 1991 The Pratt Art Institute of L.A. invited me to do my thing near the gallery. The HOLLYWOOD MONSTERS PUBLIC POEM ensued, with the assistence of Blaine, Bory, Carrega & Sarenco. I fabricated a huge tv "screen", writing the word "monster" hundreds of times shaping the image of a giant angel on the glass. We dragged it out onto the busy freeway, and there staged a conversation by speech-balloons between Kafka, Proust & Joyce on Hollywood & High Culture, sex & illusion, and the star system as a breeding ground of female monsters. It was an animated discussion and at its conclusion the team of masked literati dashed in a bunch through the screen suicidally, shattering it in your classic L.A. "highway smash-up". The traffic department was not amused as we quickly swept up the debris from the "accident", as I explained it to them.

The PUBLIC SHAMANIC CHAPEL SIX-TINE POEM was performed in 1998 with my poetic guerillero Marc Dachy & Fluxus Maître D Francesco Conz, but without the Pope's permission. I refer to the Vatican, Rome. Fourteen persons in my team, same number as in the "Creation of Adam" fresco. I intended to turn the gaze of visitors from "Heaven" above to "Terra", the shamanic habitat, below for 15 minutes, thus altering a fundamental posture of man for the first time in 5 centuries! Directly beneath the fresco, the team collapsed in positions mirroring those of the characters in the fresco, clapping on the exotic shamanic masks we had concealed, and I turned on the loudspeakers under my coat playing frantic cartoon animal roars, grunts and squeals in an updated version of shamanic communication. Marc as God stretched his index finger to Adam. 15 minutes bliss and 500 tourists staring downward until the Swiss Guard marched me off for interrogation by a bemused and urbane cardinal.

One fine June day of 2003 I enacted the PUBLIC SURVEILLANCE POEM in Paris where I saw too many cameras in the Metro system. Karen Moller my companion was my main collaborator, and friends Marc Dachy, Ester Ferrer, Tom Johnson, Liliane and Youri Vincy, Ignacio Gomez de Liano, Charles Dreyfus, Jacques Donguy Jacqueline Sigaar, Françoise Janicot, Emile Oger & Adrienne Larue carried 77 mirror-Eyes (God's) at the tips of wands, and with them peered at the crowds in the metro but especially into the cameras reflecting their image back to the watching controllers My ambulatory loudspeaker broadcast the songs of all the birds of the world as the mirror-eyes bobbed & floated above our heads. As we paraded through the tunnels of the République underground, I chanted the words "regarde qui regarde qui" (look at who is looking at who is looking at who) and in conclusion we all got on the train home singing "regarde qui" accompanied by an underground jazz band!

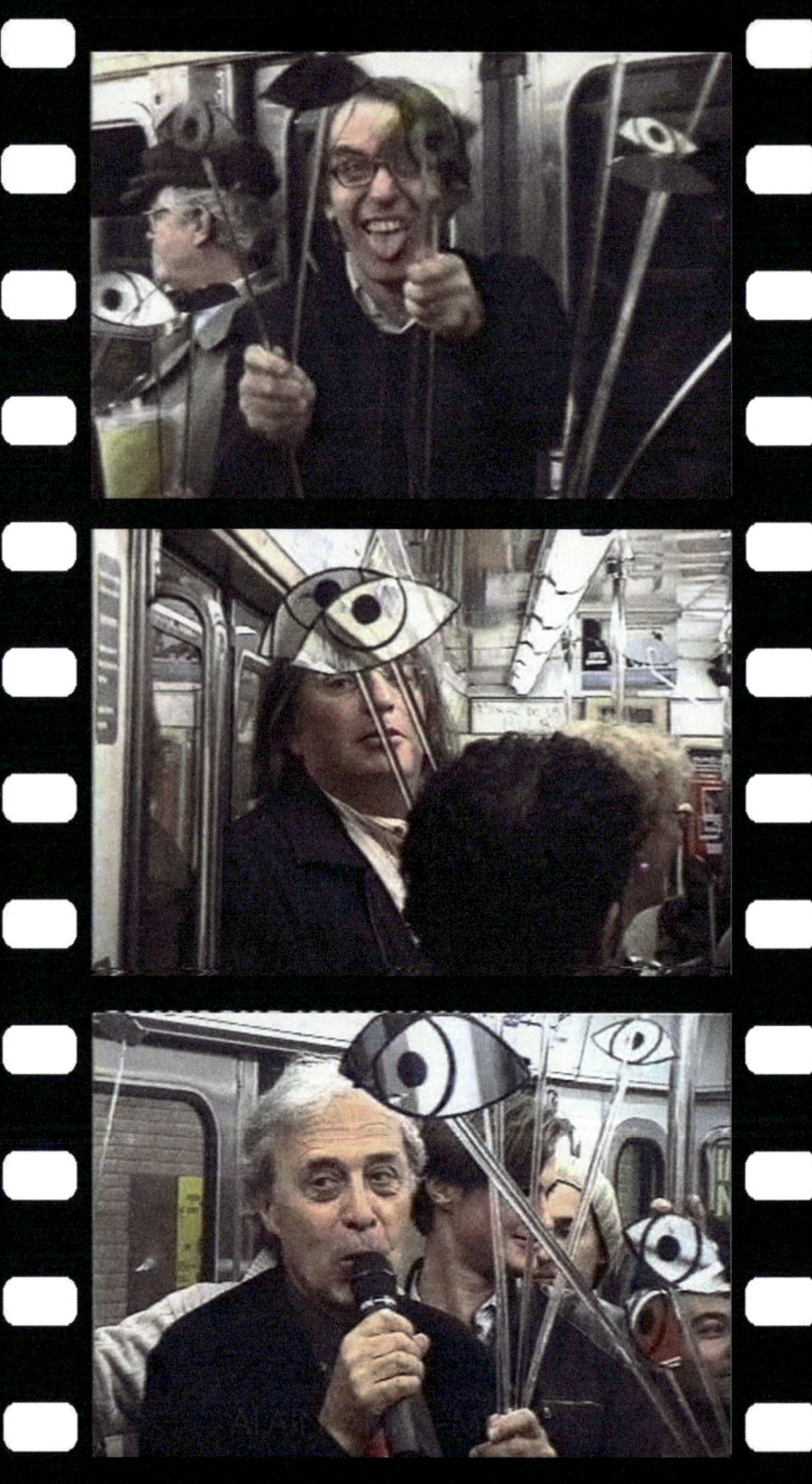

The Krikri Fetival of Ghent invited me to do an event in their fair city in 2007. Now Ghent held the archives of my great friend Paul De Vree with whom I co-edited de Tafelrond in Antwerp in 1968; and since Paul was a great friend of the ladies, I decided to dedicate a PUBLIC PANTIES POEM to him and dress Ghent in lingerie! A suitcase stuffed with panties & bras, I in the uniform of the Belgian army, one wing black with Al Quaeda emblem, the other the American flag with stars and stripes, wearing a gas-mask and carrying a boom box playing New Orleans funeral blues in his memory, I proceeded to glue panties and bras and to put inflated white rubber gloves left and right above in a gesture of female surrender on political and cultural statues, on trees, on the Modern Museum portal, at the library housing his archive, finally dressing the naked androgenous statues at the fountain, glory of the city, where a female officer--naturally--halted the Elegy in spite of my flirtatious plea.

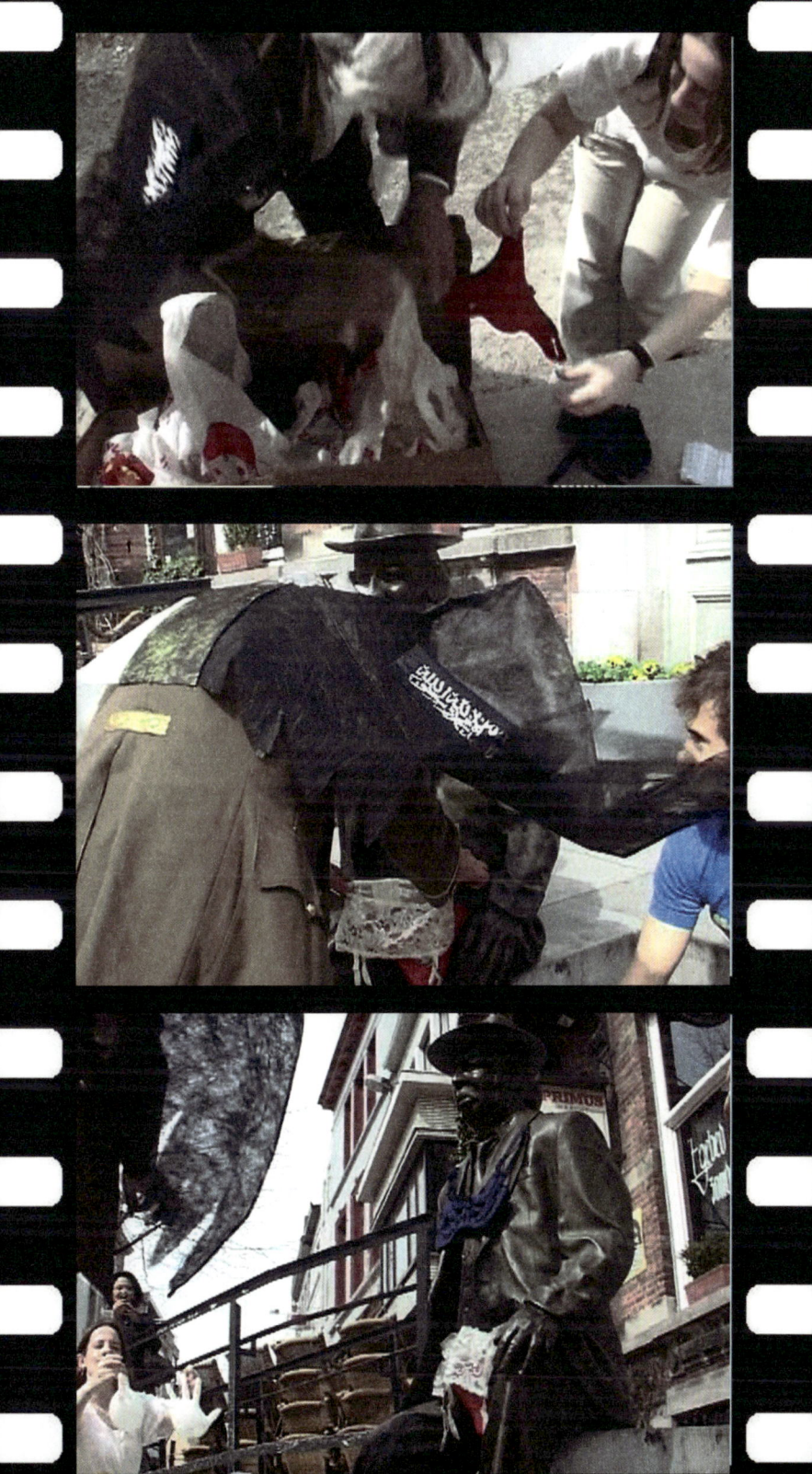

LA DERNIERE S(C)ÈNE ("supper" and "stage") was performed in 2008: the only Public Poem I say I "performed" because the theme is the (sacred) stage of the "polis". Wearing my "Magritte bowler" hat I carried 13 white chairs setting them down at three sites in the center of Nice. I sat in each of the 13 chairs one after the other raising my bowler, collecting each chair after I sat on it. In the fourth image as I sat in the center chair (the 13th!) my hat is seen aureoled in light—the Christic position. The urban dimension of the theater was dramatized when I set the chairs across a busy street, during a red light. I saluted them with my bowler and the traffic roared up nearly smashing them and me--the city as audience is no claque! My final hommage was to return the chairs to the street people who wished to reclaim their seats in the theater, and so I raised my hat to them in this public poem dedicated to the street as the last stage and the city as the final theater.

LA DERNIÈRE CÈNE or the Last Supper which I enacted in Marseille on Julien Blaine's proposal in 2008 resembled La Dernière S(c)ène superficially but was radically different in ethos and theme. I also used the 13 chairs of the apostles, but the resemblance stops there: as posed, comic and formal as was the former, this Public Poem was savage, dangerous and chaotic. Wearing a gas mask and a clown's mask under the gas mask- a bowler hat, a dark coat & carrying a wine botle and a loaf of bread (christic elements), I spread the disciples' chairs throughout the street in the stormy night weather and the heavy traffic, and occupied one chair after the other, drinking and eating, and shouting at busses and cars, and only at the end removed the gas mask revealing the clown's mask, and proceeded to address the crowd through speech-balloons announcing Apocalypse and proclaiming the advent of the Last Theater.

Alain Arias-Misson: The Belgian Years

In 1967 Alain Arias-Misson returned from the United States to Brussels, the city where he was born. He found himself as an artist midstream in the European protest movement of May '68 (Paris) and Provo (Amsterdam, Antwerp). The influence of concept art and happenings is perceivable. Furthermore a counter-current was developing in Western Europe in opposition to the influential Pop Art and Minimalism which dominated the art market. Documenta in 1968 in the West German city of Kassel was characterized by this invasion of the museums and galleries of Europe. It quickly became evident that European artists intended to preserve their identity in the framework of modern art history, which at that time had developed mainly in Belgium, Holland, Germany, Italy and Spain. The anti-American position was largely driven by the artist and philosopher Joseph Beuys, and by a political world exasperated by the imperialist trend. In the beginning of the previous century a modernism had been founded in Europe, on the other hand, that was apparently seen by Americans as « above their heads ».

In Flanders the experimental poet, Paul van Ostayen (1896–1928), already in the early years of the 20th century, had initiated a poetry in which the conventional word order was replaced by geometrically combined letters in the manner of visual and phonetic poetry. His influence on « concrete poetry » was unmistakably significant.

Paul De Vree (1909–1982), writer, essayist and art historian, as well as artist, had pointed out Arias-Misson to me in the early seventies as an innovator and fellow-combatant in the activities about visual poetry-the response to linear poetry and the new concept art. I visited him in his apartment/atelier at 78 Mettewielaan in Brussels. The artist gave an impression of self-assurance but the American influence on his view of the arts was apparent in the background. In 1973 I took the decision to show some of his works in my exhibition « Conceptual Art » at the Korrekelder Theater in the city of Brugge, one of the most important world art centers of the Middle Ages. Among the other artists that I selected were Klaus Groh, Jiri Valoch, Hugo Heyrman, Yoshio Nakajima, Petr Stembera and Paul De Vree. My intention through this show was to emphasize the broad interpretation of the idea of « concept art ». This was largely characterized, as I saw it, more by the creative possibilities inherent in an « art of the idea », as I defined it, than in the concept art that was being produced at the time. Indeed, in the view of Seth Siegelaub conceptual art was restricted to the idea or concept itself. In the spirit of the European approach, I felt that the art of the idea should also have a visual face.

Arias-Misson's contribution consisted of three photographic works on canvas. The influence of Belgian surrealism is unmistakable in the staging of the figures. The photographs show cartoon balloons in the bodies of the characters as an expression of their thought. I considered these as a form of narrative photo-works, which I situated in the entourage of a group of French artists like Paul Armand Gette, Jochen Gerz and Didier Bay. The artistic impulses of Arias-Misson participated in the influences of the times. His double nationality, with the originality of an American background set in the above-described context, was not always to the taste of the Flemish public. But the environment, first of Antwerp and later of Brussels, no doubt had a balancing effect on him—he integrated fully into the West European art milieu. Art has no nationality but it is subject to influences of urban and regional societies. And meanwhile his friendship with Paul De Vree thrived and doubtless further affected the evolution of his thought. His activity as collaborator of the review De Tafelronde without a doubt is apparent in this regard. But Arias-Misson also came into contact with art centers in advance through his collaboration with Celbeton in Dendermonde, with VECU in Antwerp, with New Reform in Aalst, as well as the famous Jeanne Buytaert gallery of Antwerp, all of which made up the avant-garde scene in Flanders at that time. In 1967 at the exhibition of « Visual and sound poetry » organized by Paul De Vree in Celbeton, two photographic works of Arias-Misson were shown. In 1974 I took an extensive documentation of his work during the 'one day show' of the New Reform art centre in the Jan Van Eyck Academy in Maastricht, Holland.

But visual poetry was by no means Arias-Misson's final aim. His work developed independently along lines similar to Fluxus and happenings, in which art became visual through action. He developed his own language of art in public spaces: the « Public Poem ». From 1968 to 1972 he enacted four public poems in Brussels and Knokke. These venues were not happenstance. The worldly spa of Knokke had made a reputation for itself as a haven for contemporary art, centrally located at the Casino. In 1967 this reputation was enhanced by the much talked about happening of the Frenchman Jean-Jacques Lebel, and Yoko Ono, living in London at the time, on the occasion of the Experimental Film Festival. It brought the two artists, who presented themselves in the nude on the stage during the Miss Festival election, legal proceedings and a prison sentence followed by a ban from Belgium for the duration of the validity of the sentence. In May of 1968, the Palace of Fine Arts of Brussels was occupied by artists under the leadership of Marcel Broodthaers; a poet who became a visual artist when he processed his unsold books of poetry to sculpture: 'Le Pense-Bête' (1964). In one of his letters to Arias-Misson (then living in Spain), De Vree speaks of this stormy political period, and at the same time the first signs of a dual Belgian society were becoming apparent. For that matter, it is notable that Arias-Misson's poetic actions were limited to Brussels and Flanders, even though his father was originally from Wallonia.

Solidly within the sphere of provocative action, Arias-Misson enacted his first public poem, VIETNAM, outside the Botanical Gardens of Brussels, a historical site which refers to a Brussels of the past of architectural distinction and fashion. Arias-Misson installed the seven letters of VIETNAM consisting of human-sized letters wrapped in surgical tape and sprayed with blood in the center of the square. The Vietnam Poem stood fully in the context of his anti-militaristic position as a draft-resister in the United States. The poem had a multi-level bearing-political, autobiographical and linguistic/esthetic. This position provided moreover a sharp perception of the men and women living and working in the city as the essence of society.

It became quickly obvious that Arias-Misson sought a broad public audience with his public poems. In 1972 I observed one of his poetic interventions at the Place de Brouckère of Brussels, at that time one of the sites at the heart of the city most densely packed with pedestrians. At a stone's throw from there in May 1967 the Innovation Department Store burned down with 323 dead. From the steps of the opera building of the Muntschouwburg, participants arrived at the public event among the masses of people moving in the various directions, which Arias-Misson had reconnoitred and observed in advance. He wanted to give a syntax to the complex structure of movement, but also gave expression to a mental theater (one of his principal socio-esthetic categories) of human intuition. The enactment of the poetic action took place not by chance on a Monday morning at 9 am, a time when the city returns to life. It is also striking that in his invitation sent to participants it was made clear that the public poem might take minutes or hours to carry out.

On the occasion of this particular action, Arias-Misson handed out pamphlets in which the complex structure of the behaviour of people in public spaces was set forth, taking as its point of departure « Chomsky's generative grammar in the street ». This may perhaps have been the most conceptual public poem based on a clear « performance » that Arias-Misson has realized.

Intimately present in all his public poems is the connection with urban spaces. Even Knokke, the little spa by the North Sea, exhibits the symptoms of urban behaviour. The Brussels jet set went there for a swim, and on a sunny day it could rival with Nice. On the occasion of the Knokke Poetry Festival in 1972, the Brussels artist Arias-Misson, requested the participation of like-minded artists at the international festival to stride into the sea with him. The artist's « poets » ritually soaked the human-sized letters P O E M X in the salt water, as a metaphor of the fusion or « osmosis » of world and word in the new poetics, as the foam rubber letters absorbed the salt water. We might characterize the event as a « sacred » event, the baptism and naming of the public poem.

The presence of Arias-Misson in the art milieu of Flanders did not pass unremarked. There were further events, which drew a tighter bond with the immediate suroundings. In 1969 De Tafelronde published his « Signs for Everyday » in which he reconstructed a trip through the city of Brussels set down in the most ordinary of photographs (tram stops, garbage, postmen) and through the flattest tongue-in-cheek commentary. This procedure was doubtless close to Fluxus, which launched such experiments in contradiction with established values. There is no doubt that his thinking was as close to Fluxus and happenings as to concrete and visual poetry, his « official » context. Arias-Misson quickly came to the conclusion that the processes involved in the enactment of the public poem possessed a deeper value than the Works themselves in the end.

It is also striking that a sort of disguise is present in a number of works: Groucho Marx moustache and eyebrows at first, masks later. Is that the consequence of the partly illegal life-view that he adopted (most public poems break city laws), or did the influential artist James Ensor (one of Arias-Misson's favorite artists) play a role here? In his correspondence with Paul De Vree we read that Arias-Misson paid an important visit to Ostende as birthplace of Ensor. Tintin (or Kuifje in Dutch) will play a masked role in the next, very provocative public poem that Arias-Misson has prepared for Brussels in 2013. And Marcel Broothaers also disguised his nose with white paint for his film Un Voyage à Waterloo (1969).

The itinerary of Arias-Misson through Brussels is as interesting as his transient domiciles from New York to Algiers, from Barcelona and Madrid to Antwerp and Brussels, and then to Venice and Paris and back to Brussels. He was born in Sint-Pieters-Woluwe on December 11, 1936, became a refugee to the United States (New York) in 1939, then from 1952 to 1954 returned to study in Belgium, until he returned to the United States for the rest of his studies at high school and Harvard University. In the seventies in Brussels he lived in five different domiciles. He presently resides at Zennestraat. Clearly, he cannot tear himself away from Brussels! We strolled through the streets of the capital of Europe recently with the sense of a close bond. This led to a renewed collaboration. In 2010, he collaborated in an 'in situ' project with talented Young Belgian artists in the French town of Paraza, which I organized, and in the « Spirits of Internationalism » show at M KHA, Van Abbe Musem and others. After so many years he has kept all his originality.

Roger D'Hondt